Comfort & Joy:

Stories of Hope, Meditations for Happiness

By Sylvia M. Ewing
Photos by Sylvester Harvey Jr.

First published by Dog Ear Publishing
4010 W. 86th Street, Ste H
Indianapolis, IN 46268
www.dogearpublishing.net

ISBN: 978-1-4575-1220-9

This book is printed on acid-free paper.

Printed in the United States of America

Dedication

"The light that shines above the heavens and above this world, the light that shines in the highest world, beyond which there are no others—that is the light that shines in the hearts of men."

From The Upanishads, Chadogya

For my daughter and best editor Eve. For Jan for her example and for Marti of unflagging faith. Thanks also to Sylvester, Matthew, Kriyananda and everyone who shared their story. Peace and much love.

Table of Contents

INTRODUCTION

People believe that it is through suffering that people grow. But if you become aware, look around and study history, you will see that no degree of suffering brings unfoldment. It brings degradation. People can adjust to anything and everything—even to pain and suffering. Learn through joy and happiness, now.

-Goswami Kriyananda

Ask my friend Aaron how he's doing, and he'll always respond the same way—"This is the best day of my life!" And you know what? He means it.

Aaron is one of those people who has found a way to be happy, pretty much all of the time. Observing the way he lives his life inspired me, so I set out to speak with other happy people I know. What is their secret? What do they have in common?

The first thing I learned was that these folks share the ability to be content and still; to find their inner voice in the midst of the distractions that swirl around them.

I believe we can learn from the positive stories of others, and when we learn from them, we honor them.

Why I Wrote this Book

I was first prompted to investigate the link between meditation and happiness for the simple reason that meditation has improved my life and I'd like to share my happiness.

Let me be clear—I'm no saint. I live in the modern world, not in a monastery or a cave. I've been around for a while, and that's a good thing. I've been in public broadcasting on both sides of the microphone, a single mom, oldest child, a media trainer, and fitness instructor. I've held jobs from receptionist to office manager, management consultant to makeup artist. I've spent my career working with diverse individuals and institutions. I love telling stories on television, radio, on the page, and on the stage.

It was easy for me to gravitate towards "happy" people. I wanted to pull out that joy that I knew existed within them for myself and others, so I conducted some interviews, using the oral tradition of fellow Chicagoans whom I admire. As I wrote and lived every day, I felt lucky to share my interviewees' stories. I'm not saying that the folks in this book are perfect either, but I have seen firsthand how they carry themselves, and I believe they have character and positive attitudes. We can benefit from just witnessing this.

I also realized that years of daily meditation made it pretty hard for me to sustain a bad mood. I'm still learning, and I have many fears to let go. But I'm happy, because second-by-second I'm really all right. When my condo flooded a few years ago and I lost nearly everything, I understood that what we have does not define who we are. I realized that there is really no reason to waste precious moments of consciousness being unhappy. And if you believe as I do, that there are no random acts, that we are all connected, then your being happy will help all those in your world.

How to Use this Book

I've met so many people who say the same things: "I can't meditate!" "I have trouble concentrating." "I'm bored by yoga." But the fact is that there is a style of meditation for every personality and a technique for every mood! Let go of your preconceived notions of meditation and together let's try to discover the best meditation techniques to unearth your eternal happiness.

<u>*Comfort and Joy: Stories of Hope, Meditations for Happiness*</u> is organized in what I hope will be a useful format. In each chapter, I share the story of a person who opened up to me about his or her faith and source of comfort. This is their point of view and I'm grateful to them for trusting me with it. Following each story is a lesson on a different style of meditation for you to try. The techniques are from my teacher training. This should show you a variety of options to help you get started, or to enhance your meditation journey. My interviewees come from diverse backgrounds because this book is concerned with spirituality, not religion.

In the 21st century, the faith practices and traditions of old still have meaning, and the ancient wisdom of yoga can be a way out of the malaise many of us face in the modern world. At the core, my goal is to inspire you and give you the tools you need to discover a meditation technique that works for you.

There are a number of ways you can make *Comfort and Joy: Stories of Hope, Meditations for Happiness* a part of your daily practice. You can read it from start to finish, trying the different meditation techniques as you go along. Or, you can review the meditation techniques and create or enhance your own practice. Later, when you need encouragement, pick one of the stories of the spiritual travelers just to give you a bit of motivation. Or, just open the book to a random section every morning. Whatever your choice, I hope you will find a lesson relevant to your life.

If you find some small benefit from this book, I thank you. If you are happier, so too will be others in your world. Meditation is extremely helpful for teens, those who are grieving, people who are ill, and others who need a way to travel beyond the confines of the physical world; to find comfort and joy deep inside the soul. I particularly hope these teachings will help those who make time in their lives to serve others. I'd like to comfort parents, encourage teachers, renew caregivers, and bring peace to the peacemakers.

Comfort and Joy: Stories of Hope, Meditations for Happiness contains my views and personal perspective, the perspective of my interviewees in their stories, and meditation techniques I learned as a certified instructor. As I've said, meditation has helped me to be happy and improved my life in every way.

In this book, I will share much more information on what meditation is, and what it is not. I set out to provide an accessible guide to help you start or strengthen your personal meditation practice. The result is a small book with a big gift of positive, real life stories and actual meditation techniques.

My training as a certified meditation teacher—along with decades of observing life, spiritual searching, and listening—has resulted in my desire to share techniques for maintaining joy and living a balanced life. In the end, the people who shared their stories on these pages are listening for and listening to that inner voice that pull of the Universe that lets life unfold and puts us on our path to greater enlightenment. Let us learn from them, and let us be joyful together.

Sylvia's stepping stones to happiness...

Happiness comes from self mastery—being aware of, and responsible for what we feel. Happiness does not come and go—it is always within us, waiting to be noticed!

CHAPTER 1:

Definition, Benefits, and Bliss

Being happy is the birthright that we find hardest to accept. After all, isn't it generally one's duty to weather the slings and arrows of life? Aren't we most impressed with stories of people who face adversity, who suffer, and come out on the other side of their pain? Is this the stuff the path of life is made of? Well, yes and no. The single greatest insight I've had in my adult life was the realization that we are here to learn, and we can learn through joy as easily as we can learn from hard knocks.

For me, meditation is first and foremost transcending thought. It is about getting rid of your worries over work, bills, kids, lovers, and the habits that come with life on earth. These concerns and negative thoughts block our ability to be happy, because they block awareness of the moment. Using meditation removes this barrier so that the happiness that is always there can then unfold. Realize that meditation is beyond the concept of "stress relief." It is about spirituality more than religion; more than belief, it is about direct experience and wisdom. Meditation is the art of letting go of negative patterns in the mind. Meditation helps us remember who we really are as spiritual beings, and leads us to maturity and wisdom. Meditation is *turning inward*, understanding our true nature, and *turning upward* towards a higher awareness of universal truth and universal connection. Meditation is not simply concentration, although concentration is a stage in the meditative process. Concentration is the effortful holding of the mind to one thing. In meditation, we are trying to get the mind to work *without* effort— my guru or master teacher, Goswami Kriyananda, calls this a state of full attention without tension.

Meditation removes negativity, hate, fear, and jealousy, so that we can be happy. Meditation keeps us in the moment, and also allows us to change the past and the future, by changing our attitude towards people and events. Take a second to reflect on this! Meditation quiets the mind so we can make wise choices, see situations clearly, and have perspective. Meditation releases chemicals and hormones in the brain and body so that we can be enthusiastic, energetic, and feel younger. Anyone who has experienced a regular practice understands the anecdotal evidence of the positive benefits of meditation, and there are many studies on the impact of meditation on various parts of the brain. Dr. Herbert Benson of Harvard pioneered research on the impact of Transcendental Meditation decades ago. The most exciting research I see coming in at this time involves Richard Dawson, a University Of Wisconsin-Madison neuroscientist, and the Dalai Lama! Their Center for Investigating Healthy Minds will use brain imaging technology on Buddhist monks to learn how their meditation training affects mental health.

However, in simple terms meditation helps us align our inner and outer worlds. My interviewees, and most happy people, see and feel our connection to the Universe. They are spiritual people with a belief in something greater than themselves, but also in their power to improve change and survive.

I've been meditating off and on for about 30 years, and over time I've turned it into a daily habit. In the past I practiced a mixture of chanting, visualizing, and simply trying to achieve peace of mind. Slowly I've come to rely on meditation to allow insight and direction to come into my life. I now understand the art and science of meditation, thanks to training, and I have not missed a day of meditation in many years. I've meditated in my car after my condo flooded in a devastating storm, I've meditated sitting quietly in my airplane seat on international flights, and I've meditated on the lakefront at dawn. In other words, I don't miss my practice. My friend Tom Mula says it best—"An action repeated becomes a habit; a habit repeated becomes a life." So act like the person you want to become, and it will be so.

Meditation is a part of the yogic process. It is tool for self-awareness and self-control that is adjunct to many styles of yoga and stress reduction techniques. I follow a form called Kriya yoga, which a focus on service to others and spiritual maturity. I also practice Hatha yoga, which is very well known because many people use it as a form of exercise. I have also found that Bikram, which is performed in a hot room, suits me as well.

My guru has said that meditation quiets the mind so that we may remember the joy of existence. I use meditation to connect me to a sense of awareness of that eternal joy.

More people than ever take yoga class in some shape or form, and many of you may have already tried meditation. Can we bring the benefits of the studio or yoga mat out into the world? Can we make the connection between our most spiritual inner world and everyday life? Yes we can.

First Steps to Meditation

Before we begin, here is an overview of the technique you can use to prepare for all types of meditation. This technique echoes ancient form, but also helps to address the timeless search for stress reduction and concentration. There are modifications to this process, as well as a reason for each element, but let's keep it simple for now and explain all the esoteric symbolism you may encounter as you journey into meditative practice.

Relaxation. Be comfortable! In the style of yoga that I adhere to, this is key. Sit with your spine as erect as possible so that your breath and your energy can flow freely. You might sit in a chair and put a cushion under your feet to create a more comfortable alignment. You may sit on a cushion, or sit on the floor. The floor is ideal, and you should have a special blanket or small rug made of cotton or wool that you use just for this purpose. You don't need to try to sit in some advanced pose, or in your mass-media image of the perfect sitting yogi. Yes, I know we live in a world where people are copyrighting yoga postures, but you don't need to concern yourself with one-upmanship. This is a relationship between you and you. There is no competition, just day-by-day awareness. What you do with ease one day may be a little harder on a different day, but there is always growth because you are opening your inner pathway to awareness of the moment and happiness.

Conscious breathing. Breathe mindfully. Inhale, pause. Exhale slowly. You might connect your breath to a simple thought such as I am calm, or all is well. We are rarely aware of breathing unless we are in distress, but controlling the breath helps control the mind. That's why observing the breath is our first meditation exercise.

Close your eyes. This is a good time to make sure you are relaxed. Soften the jaw, relax the tongue, and let it float between the teeth.

Focused attention. Pretend that you are looking between the eyes at the bridge of your nose, then let your gaze move slightly upward. Relax, don't stare or strain—just make a gentle effort in that direction.

Visualization. At this stage, you will set the intention in your mind to be a person who can relax and be happier with meditation. Even if you start to think "I can't do that," you will tell yourself that all is well in your world.

Concentration. This is the stage of meditation that is often confused with meditation itself. It is helpful to have this ability no matter what, and we'll learn the ways to have effective pre-meditative concentration.

Meditation. Aha! After all of these steps, you will experience a moment of letting go; of calm and peace. Serenity, equanimity, contentment. At first this might be only a few seconds, but regardless of the length of time, this is meditation, and it is the intensity—not the duration—that matters. Enjoy the short meditation while it lasts and stop when it's time to stop.

We are actually supposed to be happy. We neglect to realize that we owe it to our friends and our families to be happy. Meditation makes it easier. Meditation is a way to gain and sustain a positive outlook on life, and therefore to be happy. Lao Tzu and the Tao Te Ching, the Yoga Sutras of Patanjali, biblical Psalms, the Koran, and the Kabala all show the benefit of being that "Pollyanna" who sees the best in everything; as one of my friends puts it, sees the glass not as half empty but as full and overflowing. I hope to help you see that you are always one thought away from reaching happiness.

CHAPTER 2

Breeze Richardson

Breeze is a young mother of two boys, and works in radio. She finds happiness in silence and in service to others. This is her story...

I was raised as a member of the Religious Society of Friends—known to many as Quakers—and continue to practice my faith as an adult. My parents were both raised pretty secularly, and I think like many parents, wanted to find a religious community, a spiritual home for their children. I'm the oldest of four children, so I was the one that prompted them to begin that quest.

We lived in a little Illinois community called Sycamore, outside of DeKalb, Illinois, and they found a Quaker meeting in DeKalb to start attending. I have memories of the meeting house, of being there as a child. When I was about 11 we moved to the Kansas City area; this is the spiritual community from where I have the most memories. This is where I grew up and went on to actually attend a Quaker boarding school for part of my high school years. Later, I became active nationally in the Religious Society of Friends, and then it was only natural that when I came here to Chicago that I would seek them out. I have been a member of the 57th Street Meeting in Hyde Park for over six years.

A Faith that Works for All Ages

I don't know much about other faiths, but it's very true that in Quakerism there is a non-dogmatic, individual relationship with one's spirituality. I think a lot of the adult community struggles, somewhat, on how to approach their youth, especially their teenagers, since we feel strongly that every individual has the right and responsibility to create that spiritual path for themselves. It puts you somewhat in a bind as to how to mentor your young people, and how to shape the environment in which they can ask spiritual questions for themselves, and come to whatever determination they want to come to. I, like a lot of high school and college kids, wasn't as active in those years as I was when I came here to Chicago in my twenties. I think the transition to a new place was really helpful for me in not only seeking out a spiritual community when I arrived in Chicago, but really finding a home that became a significant part of my daily life.

Probably one of the greatest gifts that Quakerism has given me is a belief in me—not scripting, a creed, or a liturgy. Nothing dictates to me what I should believe and how that should shape my daily life. Leaving those decisions and that interpretation up to me really empowered me to find that place for myself, and to trust and believe in it.

Coping with Challenges

I'm usually my worst critic, so my hard days usually come from me feeling like I didn't do my best or respond in the best way to a challenging, stressful situation. I've got this incredible foundation of silent worship though, of inward reflection that allows me to analyze a situation, learn from the situation, believe in myself that I can make mistakes, and improve the next time around. I'm able to move forward knowing that I'll continue to be that person who gets to push myself, then be able to accept my success or my failures. My relationship with the divine is very internal, and I think that allows me to critique myself and then confidently walk through that situation with authority, because I'm not looking to a minister or a pastor or a priest or a parent to give me that sense of validation.

I also recognize that each challenge is a moment in time. Quakers definitely hold the present moment to be of utmost concern and value. That's something that is really important to me. When I'm at my best I'm fully in the moment, and not thinking ahead of myself.

Outlook for Life

Though there are many branches of Quakerism, my branch, known as the "un-programmed branch," is very non-pastoral. We don't preach. It's really about one's individual experience. There is a concept of concentric circles that really guides me in my spirituality—I ask myself, how am I doing? What needs to be addressed or discerned or ultimately corrected about me and how I'm walking through this world? How is my immediate family? How is my husband and how is my child? Do they need to be nurtured? Then, what about my extended family? What about my work family? What about my spiritual community, my city, and my world? I move through these concentric circles, and then I go back to where I started.

I realize that starting from the individual, moving out, and then going back again means that you could spend all day, every day just trying to fix the things that you feel could be improved in your life. Since there is so much else to do in a day, I think there is also something to be said for just rising above your problems, instead of meditating on them—realizing that the clock is going to keep ticking, and this day is going to end. The next day is going to start, and it's all about what is right in front of you.

I'm also a big fan of treating yourself, whether that means a homemade smoothie, a quick nap, taking time to write in a journal, or whatever it is that really makes you realize there is more in the moment than whatever you're facing. After you treat yourself, you can come back to the issue at hand with new eyes, and realize that things can't be fixed immediately. By seeing clearly whatever is troubling you, you can move into a better place and take the first step to addressing it.

I think that one of the things Quakerism has given me, one of the main reasons I continue to practice communally, is that it forces me to carve out a space that's all about me sitting in that silence, supported by others doing the same. Silent worship is the foundation upon which we practice, but it can also be those ten minutes in the shower, taking a walk around the block, or just sitting in a space that's quiet. I think that we're really distracted by a lot of things that are in our environment, and it's hard to just sit with your thoughts in today's day and age. But when I do, I always walk out of those situations so much more rejuvenated, and feeling celebratory of the people and the experiences that I'm so blessed to have in my life. I've given myself the space to acknowledge my life. I think to find time to just be with yourself and realize all the amazing things that you have is something that you completely control. It's a joy that you can create.

May quietness descend upon my limbs,
My speech, my breath, my eyes my ears...

—The Upanishads (Ancient Hindu spiritual texts)

CHAPTER 3

Technique— The First Steps of Meditation

Meditation may be a mystical science, but there are practical steps to make it meaningful in your life. Breeze Richardson is a person who finds comfort and joy in stillness and reflection, therefore her story was a good introduction to the first steps of meditation.

Breathing is transparent. Breathing is a real barometer for our emotions and how we feel—it tells us what's happening in our unconscious. Meditation on the breath is not intended to control the breathing, but to *observe* the breathing. Letting go of control of breath allows us to let go of other tensions, and let our life unfold. When we do this, we are also better able to accept how others let their lives unfold without trying to control them.

Meditating on the Breath

Observing the breath is a key technique in helping you to let go, calm down, master your mind, and control the body. The Sanskrit word for it is "pranayama," and it means breath awareness and control. In some techniques the goal is to simply breathe; in others, the breath is controlled. This technique applies a level of control in the beginning.

1. Make the body still and comfortable. Lift up your shoulders and let them fall a few times. Ask yourself if you are ready to meditate. Many of my students find it easier to feel the three-part breath used in this technique by lying down the first time. If seated, you can rest your hands on your knees. More advanced practitioners also use mudras, which are ways of positioning the fingers that sages say are linked to the chakras, or energy channels, of your body. According to eastern philosophy, these energy points run from the pelvic area to the throat. The most commonly known mudra is having the fore fingers and thumbs touching. But having the hands on the knees if seated, or the palms facing up with the arms close to the body if lying down is fine.

2. Visualize bringing your energy from your arms and legs into the core of your body, to your spine. You can do this by picturing an arrow above your body that you move from your toes, up your legs, into the base of your spine. Then from your fingers, and again into your spine.

3. Close your eyes and let them focus at the bridge of your nose and then upward. Observe your breath until it is quiet. Watch with detachment and don't try to control it.

4. Inhale deeply through the nostrils. Feel yourself filling your abdomen completely. Let the abdomen expand as you inhale; let it rise and

then contract with the breath a few times until you get the feel of it. This is part one of the three-part breath.

5.   Continue the abdominal breathing. Now, feel your inhalation rising from the abdomen up the back, filling out the area below your bottom rib, where your kidneys are located. As you inhale and the breath rises, feel it pushing against your back. Breathe several times concentrating on the two parts of this breath: filling your abdomen, and moving up your back.

6.   Feel your breath coming up until it reaches just below your collar bone. Take your time and enjoy the fullness of these three parts. As you exhale, reverse the process, with your awareness moving from under the collar bone to the abdomen. Concentrate on these moves. If other thoughts come in, gently but firmly move the mind back to the breath. Quiet the mind to focus on nothing but the breath.

As you relax you should automatically soften the breath. Your goal is to eventually move past your awareness of the technique, to your awareness of the breath coming in and the breath going out. Don't try to control it, but as you breathe in let your thoughts go to breathing in goodness and light. As you exhale let your thoughts focus on letting go and being content. You can also add a sense of lifting, or listening to the heart. You can try beginning or ending with affirmations, which we'll get to later.

7.   Eventually the body breathes itself without effort, centered on the here and now; content and detached. *This state, for however long it lasts, is when true meditation occurs.*

8.   Return to watching your breath, and breathe more deeply. Slowly and peacefully return your awareness to your physical space.

Alternate Nostril Breathing

This is a basic technique to allow you to gain conscious self-awareness, and to detach from your thoughts by mastering your body with your breath. Alternate nostril breathing is another key form of pranayama, and is considered to be a method of spiritual purification. I know that it's a sure bet when I need to calm down, and it's a wonderful tool for centering the mind to move into deeper stages of meditation, or to get a handle on my emotions. This is how to practice alternate nostril breathing:

Sitting upright, place the left hand on the left knee with the thumb and forefinger touching, and the rest of the fingers extended.

1.   All of the work is done with the thumb, the ring, and pinky finger of the right hand. Extend the right elbow out, and press the middle and index fingers tightly against the palm. Leave the thumb, ring and little fingers free.

2.   The right thumb is placed above the right nostril, and the ring and little fingers are placed against the left.

3.   To begin the alternate nostril breath inhale only through the right nostril with the left remaining closed off.

4.   When the lungs are full, press the thumb down to close off the right nostril, lift the ring and pinky fingers, and exhale slowly, steadily, and fully on the left. When the lungs are empty, inhale slowly, steadily, and fully on the left.

5. Close off the left nostril and lift the thumb to inhale on the right, and then again exhale on the right.

6. Continue 5-7 times, and end with an exhalation on the left.

Meditate for as long as you desire and as long as you can. Do it for a few seconds at a time several times a day, or cultivate a longer practice once or twice a day. However, in the beginning, keep it short. Many are surprised to hear me say that two or three minutes of meditation is ideal to start. *The key factors are intensity and intent, not length of time.* You want to train your mind to view meditation as desirable, as a gift and not a task.

When to Meditate

- If possible, try to meditate at the same time in the same place every day, especially for the first 21 days or so. This is important to help establish a routine.
- The dawn is said to be the most auspicious time. This window between night and day is a time when it is easier to find balance, but if meditating after work or at high noon is when you can practice, do what feels right for you. Remember that the best time is any time that works for you!
- Don't meditate on a full stomach. Your body has to work to digest your food, which could cause discomfort.

Create Your Environment

- A comfortable and beautiful space is conducive to a good practice. Some people have an entire room set up with pillows and art and whatever else inspires them to feel peaceful. Other people practice just as well using a space like a dresser top or bookshelf that is dedicated as a place to keep whatever they use for their meditation. In the end, the goal is to signal your mind that in this space, or before this place, lies the portal beyond your surface world. Natural light, and colors like yellow and orange always make me feel better; these can also be an important tool to cheer you up and remind you of your blessings. I even feel better when I use certain incense! These are simple ways to lift your energy and clean up your aura, which is an energy that is connected to every life form.

- It is important that you make your place of meditation comfortable, clean, and special. Careful use of candles, incense, pictures, flowers, and other symbols that are important to you can create a beautiful space, set the stage, and signal to your mind that it is time to meditate.
- Wear comfortable clothes. I agree with those who believe that everything has an energy field around it—an aura—that reflects our mind-set, attitude, and consciousness. The first impressions we give and receive, and the good feeling or unpleasantness that the company of certain people brings, are all connected to the aura. If you wish to meditate after just coming in from work, take a shower and then put on sweats or pajamas that you set aside for meditation. This will reduce your "work energy", and prevent it from entering your meditation space. Personally, I like to take an after work shower to remove that built up "work energy", whether I plan to meditate or not. When I meditate in the morning I just wear whatever I slept in.

- Music is **not** used in this technique. Now, I like to get down with the best, and I also like to use music to help me to relax. In fact, certain music gives me the energy to keep going when I'm tired, and some music helps me set a tone of peace and harmony in my house. I love the Buddha Lounge series, and Stevie Wonder's Inner Visions. Earth Wind and Fire can be downright esoteric. But when I meditate I want to hear my inner voice. I suggest that you save the music for another time and tune into the rhythm of your heart and the song of your breath when you meditate.

When you are inspired by some great purpose, some extraordinary project, all your thoughts break their bonds: your mind transcends limitations, your consciousness expands in every direction, and you find yourself in a new, great and wonderful world.

—Patanjali (an Indian sage or sages who lived sometime in the first three centuries before Christ, and is credited with organizing the basis for all yoga with his yoga sutras)

CHAPTER 4

Aaron Freeman

Aaron Freeman is a comedian and writer in his early fifties. He is African-American and Jewish, and the father of twins. He finds joy and happiness in art and in creating a lifestyle that suits his needs. This is his story...

Variety from Day One

I've been curious and passionate about different beliefs all of my life. The first church I recall going to was a Mennonite church in rural Illinois. When we moved to Chicago, my mom, for excellent political reasons, became Catholic. Catholics were supporting civil rights, they were opposed to Richard J. Daley, and they were into education—my mother's three favorite things. I went to Catholic schools, but I rejected Catholicism when I was ten.

I think secular humanism took its place as I grew older. I chanted a Buddhist mantra because Tina Turner did it. I did a little yoga, but not really as a spiritual practice. I saw no need for religion as I became an adult. I wasn't searching for anything, but I was always trying different philosophies and was curious about everything. I had a talk show at the time, and I had a bunch of rabbis on. It was fascinating and caught my attention, and I wanted to learn more. I made my producer so crazy with my questions, that he finally told me, "You want to be a Jew, go be a Jew!" And actually, that is what I eventually did. I converted to Judaism, and that is how I've raised my twin daughters.

Comfort and Gratitude

Daily Jewish observance ameliorates the worst aspect of American life. The worst aspect of American life is that consumer culture makes us endlessly aware of what we do not have without counterbalancing that with rituals of gratitude. Observant Judaism requires that a hundred times a day you have to say to yourself, "I sure am grateful I woke up!" "I sure am grateful I got a cup of coffee!" As my ex-wife so wisely pointed out, it's not possible to be grateful and pissed off at the same time. So, to the precise extent that you do your 100 blessings a day with precise intentions, to that precise extent you are a hundred percent guaranteed to be happy. That's my biggest reason for being Jewish. There's also the fact that Judaism requires a big party in the form of Shabbat every week. It's a law—there's nothing you can do about it! You're obligated to do it! And I can assure you that makes me happy. The truth is that requiring this little party every week makes the whole week better. You're always thinking about it—What are we going to eat? What are we going to cook? Who will we invite?

My wife Sharon and I also create a comic strip every week based on that week's Torah reading. Between reading the book all the time (you might say that Jews are part of the world's most obsessive book club), and doing the party every week… well, that's your week! It is time filled with stuff that you love—food, jokes, and company! You spend half of your time planning the big party and the other half reflecting on how great last week's party was. Every time you meet someone new, it's like, "Hi, I'm Aaron Freeman. How would you like to come to Shabbat dinner?"

Getting Past Hard Times

The thing that makes a tough day better is art. That's been the case for many, many years, and it's certainly the case for Sharon and me. When you're having a bad day and you create some work that you like, it's all good, always. Spirituality is our art's inspiration. It is the root of my wife's paintings, and inspires my writing. I also work as a comedian in the Jewish community, making jokes about Judaism and the Middle East. I'm a little uncomfortable saying it's a spiritual practice, but it is spiritual in that there is a certain commitment, joy, and sincerity that you bring to it. As Oscar Wilde said, the first duty of life is to enjoy it. The second duty has yet to be discovered.

Sylvia's stepping stones to happiness...

Know what you want and do that which will get you closer to your goal. Refrain from doing that which takes you away from it. Don't wait for the perfect time to change your life—**this** is always the moment.

CHAPTER 5

Technique—"EEE" Mantra

Even though he makes it sound effortlessly fun, Aaron Freeman has a disciplined routine that allows him to carry off his fantastic and festive Shabbat dinner, week after week, without fail. To be effective, meditation must also be repetitive.

It's easier to have focus when your mind is settled. A *Mantra* is the use of repetition of sacred sounds to enter a centered state of mind. There will be more on the classic mantra OM later. One of the key goals of meditation is to empty the mind so that you can see clearly, and renew and revive your energy. The EEE mantra is a simple technique to use for this, and is very "portable." I love this technique and find it to be useful in many circumstances. I often even do it in empty elevators on my way to meetings!

Here is how to do this version of the EEE mantra:

1. Inhale quickly and deeply, through your open mouth. This is something that makes this technique a little different—most meditative breathing is done through the nostrils.

2. Now exhale and say EEE (rhymes with "see") loud and proud, tensing your muscles and making fists with your hands as you do it.

3. Stop when your voice starts to waver. Repeat three times and then notice how calm your mind is.

4. Focus on your breath, and meditate quietly for as long as you are comfortable.

Tips for Creating a Regular Practice

Making time and creating space to meditate begins with living a sane lifestyle. The key thing is to do that which makes it more likely for you to be content and happy, and to not do that which hinders your happiness and enlightenment! It's also important to get the rest and nutrition you need to generate the energy and enthusiasm for meditation. What you've put into your body, and what you put into your mind, matter.

So let's move towards establishing healthy habits...

Media Diet

Watch what your mind consumes. When I was a journalist, I often monitored two or three news stations at a time, while having one ear tuned to the radio. For work and pleasure I read two or three papers a day, plus several magazines weekly. All of this media consumption had a negative effect on my mood and my worldview.

I understand from working on the inside how much of the news we see is created by a producer trying to fill a "hole" in the evening lineup. Think carefully about your reaction to the news, movies, and websites you consume. Have a real honest conversation with yourself about how it's all working for you. What do you really enjoy, and what leaves you feeling negative? You'll be more relaxed when you limit yourself to what you really want as your only media destination, and take a break from unconscious media consumption.

Rest

- Try to get more rest or more fulfilling rest
- Go to bed at the same time every night'
- Start to settle down at least an hour before bed
- Before sleep, enjoy peaceful music, a relaxing book, or something funny
- Think of your mind as being like a toddler before bed time—don't get it all wound up!

Eating Habits

- Move towards more fruit and vegetables
- Limit highly processed foods with food colorants, additives, and chemicals
- If you choose to eat meats, limit your amount and move toward fish and poultry as opposed to red meat and pork
- Don't fall prey to marketing—figure out what is actually in your food. Read the ingredients! Even better, buy food that doesn't come in a box. No one ever had to read the ingredient list on an apple!
- Learn more about where your food comes from so you can feel good about the impact your food choices make on your body and on our planet

Make Time

A great deal of stress, impatience, and plain crabbiness manifests because we are rushed. Plan extra time to get where you need to go, and to do what you need to do!

Chill Out

Often we invite drama into our lives—some people actually become addicted to troubled situations so much that they can't feel alive *without* drama. Meditation will help you to appreciate the subtle nuances of your mind so that you will never be bored. When a problem occurs, you can handle it with maturity and patience, knowing that it is but a moment in time.

Always remember that what we do, what we say, and what we *think* in life is what really matters.

As part of my meditation teacher training, I asked myself what supports and what hurts my meditation practice. Here is what I came up with:

Supports Practice	Hurts Practice
Quiet	Tension in the home
Comfortable space	Clutter and mess
Rest	Being rushed and tired
Being content	Being embarrassed
Beauty	Lack of privacy
Supportive and spiritual people	Judgmental people
Staying home	Running around
Work-life balance	Too many projects
Focus	Being scattered

Take some time to ask yourself what will support your practice and what will obstruct it. Then analyze, and act upon what you learn.

Affirmations & Intentions

An affirmation is a phrase that gives you courage and comfort. Saying, "All is well in my world" is a favorite from author Louise Hay, and "I am loved, and I am love" is a variation of one of my favorites from Deepak Chopra, the famous doctor and mystic. Setting an intention is something one can do to set a goal: "I will personalize a plan and find a process for my mind. I will do what I need to do to make my meditation comfortable. I will maintain a lifestyle that supports meditation, and I see meditation as part of my happy life." Affirmations and intentions can be used the first thing in the morning, or before any time of challenge or opportunity. Both help us to take conscious positive action, rather than moving through the day on autopilot or letting fear lead our actions.

Sylvia's stepping stones to happiness...

We all have obstacles we have drawn into our lives, but we can also overcome them. You have no enemies. There is just you, life, and your reaction to it.

CHAPTER 6

Brenda Watson

Brenda Watson is a nutritionist, author, and entrepreneur. She has been a spiritual seeker since her teens, and follows the philosophy known as A Course in Miracles, which focuses on self-awareness and positive thinking in order to be happy. This is her story...

I was raised in the South, in a large family. My mom lost a child at six months old. He died of a kink in the intestines, which actually was a doctor's error. He was taken to the doctor with an ailment, and he died on the emergency room table. Then right after, my mom became pregnant with me. It is kind of interesting that I became a professional dealing with bowels and the colon.

My mom came from a very strict background, and from a small family of two. My dad came from a farming family of 13 children—his mother had her last child at age 50. Because of their different backgrounds, my parents were a unique couple.

My parents were kind of big partiers. Dad was an alcoholic, and my mother was obsessed with him, so I was raised in a really dysfunctional home. Mom and Dad just partied a lot, drank a lot, and fought a lot. But I've been through therapy and forgiveness, and I know they did the best they could, and I love them dearly.

Casual Religion to Enlightenment

Once in a while, we would go to church. We went on Easter because we got new dresses and shoes, but my mother shied away from a lot of religion because my uncle was a Methodist preacher, and she felt that it had been shoved down her throat.

When I was 13, I had this feeling that I had been there before. From that point on, I never really gravitated towards more traditional religious beliefs. I also learned a lot from the mother of one of my girlfriends when I was in junior high school. People at school thought she was weird because she was into things like astrology, but she was just into a different type of spirituality. It touched me.

I had a child at 16, and my family's attitude was that I had made my bed, and now I had to lie in it—I had to find my own way. This was terrifying! But I went out and worked three jobs. Then, when I was about 19, I started to really gravitate towards more spiritual principles.

A Self-Made Woman

I was raised in a prejudiced environment. I never knew anything different. I wasn't exposed to different cultures; I had such limited experiences. That's why it's kind of ironic that it was an African-American therapist who really helped me when I was struggling to figure out my life, and trying to get out of a really horrible marriage. The divorce took five years because of his inability to let go, and my inability to take the responsibility of letting go of money. I had a couple of homes and cars, and all the things that people think they want to have. Eventually, when the divorce was final, he blew up my house and my cars, so I literally had only the clothes on my back!

I lost everything I owned; I had to start new with nothing. I realized then that I wanted to do something in spirituality. I kind of felt I was guided into everything. I did not have any fears over money—I didn't have any, but I decided I was OK with it. You know, I can't say I had a vision of the end result, but I knew day to day that I was doing the right thing. God was putting people in front of me, and I paid better attention to the ones that were there for my learning purposes. I met Stan, my husband, and I worked on healing myself. I started my health business from the trunk of my car using my credit card. I worked in clinics, then had my own clinic, and continued to learn.

The first time I got up to speak in front of a group of people, talking about bowel movements and constipation, I had an awakening that this was what I was going to do to help people.

Once I started working with patients in clinics, I loved it. Working with people with colonics every day, seeing people get better, and having an effect on someone's life just really turned me on. I started speaking publicly more, and as I did I realized that that was really "being in the now." I might be talking to someone about their problem with digestion, but really what they're seeing in me is love. I'm sending them a message, whether I'm talking about detox, or digestive problems, or anything like that. What they see in me is a communication of the spirit, and they relate to this.

Defining Moments

I've been through Eckhart Tolle's *The Power of Now*, you know, I've done all of that stuff. But what was really profound for me happened a few years ago. I got really depressed right before I did my first **PBS** special. I was tired and thought, is this right thing for me, to get up on TV and talk to people? One day I told my husband, "I'm going to drive to Orlando to this conference. I don't know why, but I feel like I'm supposed to go!" I knew when I walked into this conference and sat down at a particular seminar, that it was the reason I was there. It was "A Course in Miracles," and it is what I will be studying for the rest of my life.

Finding Strength

To me, anything is possible—that is how I built my company. But I still feel anxiety, and when I do I have to just fill the bathtub, relax, and pray. I'll say, "I know right now I'm in the ego. I know it because I'm in judgment and I'm projecting fear, so what I'm going to do is I'm going to move in spirit." I say to myself, OK God, I've got that willingness right now to change the way I feel, and I just relax into it. Then, I go and read one of the messages in the Miracles course. This reflection usually puts me back into the space of feeling that everything is in perfect alignment with the Universe, and it is planned as it should be.

I have to choose what I want to feel. We all have that choice, every moment of every day. Do we choose to stay in fear and ego, or do we choose to stay in love and right mindedness? I think that the key to this question is being able to step back and be the observer of yourself. Observing one's self is the hard part, but that is the part that we all have to get to. I can really look at myself and understand what I'm feeling, and how in or out of alignment it is.

It's all about a change in perception. A miracle is just a change in perception, and you can change perception with the snap of your fingers if you want to. You have to realize this: "I am absolutely responsible for every single situation in my life. Every person I encounter every day, every single thing that happens to me, I have chosen for a reason." A lot of the time we don't see that reason today or even tomorrow, but we'll see it down the road. We have to know that God's plan for us is perfect.

Sylvia's stepping stones to happiness...

Be open to new ways to worship and relate to spirituality. Look not so much to religion, but rather to direct experience of the mystical world unfolding in your life.

CHAPTER 7

Technique—"Tarka" Reflection

Watching her mind is one of the ways that Brenda stays on track. Her faith practice helps her take negative thinking head on by using positive affirmations, and equally important, by admitting when she's not in a good emotional space. When she takes time to examine her thoughts, her attitude, and her actions she is actually engaged in a yogic technique of introspection and self-examination called Tarka.

Tarka is not a meditation, but rather a technique for reflection to help you see the contents of your mind and to look at thoughts and patterns of thoughts so that you can deal with them in a conscious way. Remember, when we are more conscious we can see life as it really is—which maybe is not as bad as our imagination sees it—or see solutions when we actually do face real challenges. This state of heightened self-awareness, Tarka, can be used to look at a part of your life, a concept of spirituality, or your mind in the moment. The process lets you see yourself when you are thinking negative thoughts in the present, or to look back honestly at your behavior and the motives behind

your actions. Use Tarka as a general check-in with yourself.

How to Practice Tarka

1. Inhale thinking "I am" exhale thinking "calm."
    for a few moments
2. Take a very deep breath, hold for a few seconds
    and release it as slowly as possible. Take a few
    moments to see how you feel.
3. Ask yourself: what did I do today? Whom did I
    help or hurt? Why did I react the way I did?
    What can I learn to make my tomorrow a little
    better than today?

Tarka is also a tool to help you deal with your
thoughts. When you are feeling bad any time of the day,
observe what you're thinking. As soon as a negative
thought comes, ask why. What is the cause? Is it internal
or external? Why am I thinking this way?

Tarka and the Reversal Technique

Tarka, like meditation, is a way of truly realizing what
is going on in our minds. If it is negative, we change it, if
it is positive, we can embrace it, and if it is strange, we can
try to understand it! I have a friend who is struggling with
her feelings towards her ex-husband. Being stuck in these
thought patterns prevents her from being happy. The past
interferes with her present. For example, she hesitates to
go to certain neighborhoods where she might see her ex,
even though friends and family who love her want to meet
her there. She is limiting her life because she does not have
control over the darker thoughts in her mind. If she were
to use Tarka, she could see these patterns more clearly.
Then my friend could use the "reversal technique" to help
her climb out of the downward spiral of negativity.

My friend could use the reversal technique like this:

- Become aware of the negative thoughts: I don't want to spend time in my old neighborhood because I might see my ex.
- Use this consciousness to think back to the moment before you became sad, or hurt, or angry: A friend is inviting me to brunch.
- Think a new thought: Let's get together and talk about my wonderful new job.

Tarka is not about judging or beating yourself up. It is about seeing clearly. Tarka can help train the mind to be introspective, to see clearly, and to be honest with yourself.

In the beginning of this book I talked about changing the past and the future. You can do this by reframing your perception. We can also learn to change the past again by changing how we look at it, by forgiving and healing, and even by seeing another's point of view. In fact, when my daughter Eve had bad dreams as a child, I always told her to imagine a happy ending. She says it helped. Not only is this a less painful way to live, it also helps us eliminate seeing ourselves as victims. Now more than ever we need to see our connection to our personal power; only you can quiet and calm your mind. But to get there, you have to be aware of the inner turmoil, fear, and other imbalances in your subconscious.

We can condition our minds to overcome negative thoughts, and tame our need to control others by achieving self-control. These affirmations from my guru Kriyananda are helpful to me:

"May I have the physical and mental strength to obtain what needs to be obtained harmoniously."

"May I have the wisdom to see life clearly, and to know what needs to be done, and to know when and how to do it...*harmoniously*."

"May I strive hour by hour to be healthier and healthier, happier and happier, and more and more content."

"This is the true joy in life: the being used for a purpose recognized by yourself as a mighty one. ...I am of the opinion that my life belongs to the whole community, and as long as I live it is my privilege to do for it whatever I can."

—George Bernard Shaw, writer and philosopher

CHAPTER 8

Santita Jackson

Santita, a singer and radio talk show host, is the oldest child of Reverend Jesse Jackson. She finds happiness, tolerance, and hope in her Baptist faith. This is her story...

I was raised in the Baptist church, or more broadly, in the African-American church institution. I was also fortunate enough to grow up when my father was in seminary at the University of Chicago. I was raised around his best friends from all races. As I grew up and his ministry developed, we would go to synagogues, temples, and other diverse places of worship. We covered all of the religions; we were never locked into one church. Just to know all of these great people of the world's religions helped to send me on my journey.

I cannot say enough about my mother; she is so spiritually curious. She grew up in the Catholic Church, and like many others, she is a lapsed Catholic. She is the wife of a minister who has had the world as his pastorate, yet she would encourage me to understand other faiths like Baha'i and Islam. In fact, my bother Yusef was going to be named Joseph, but we had a family friend who was a Muslim and said, "Name him Yusef." I think moments like this have always informed my journey.

Faith and Tolerance

My mother said, "Don't limit God, because God is limitless," so I never limited God to my experience. Some of the best Christians I know are Muslim, or Jewish, or agnostic, or animists. Knowing that we're all expressions of God helps me to gain another understanding of who I am in the world, and of where we all need to be. To realize that we're all spiritual beings and we're all having this huge journey is central to who I am. I travel so much, and I've met people who are demonized in different parts of the world, like Fidel Castro, Yasser Arafat, and Henry Kissinger. Meeting people from all over the ideological spectrum humanizes them.

When I was a child we saw Alabama Governor George Wallace standing in a door saying "Segregation now. Segregation forever!" and yet when he was shot in 1972, I arrived home from school to my mother preaching forgiveness. I knew who Wallace was because I came from a highly politicized household, and I knew he was someone who did not understand or like black people very much. But my mother pulled me aside, sat me down and said, "You know the kind of work that your father does can be kind of dangerous, and there are people who when they disagree with you, they do some bad things." She went on to explain that Wallace had been shot that day. So even though he was someone who we were not in sync with at all, the fact that someone would want to kill him was devastating. I appreciate that compassion that my parents gave me.

Looking back on it, I realize they never made political disagreements or even ideological disagreements personal. You have to understand what made people like George Wallace, and when you understand people I think it really helps you to strengthen your connection to God.

Faith over Fear

Part of my personal reality has been living with daily death threats to my father's life. Therefore, I had to get into my prayer life very early. Even when I went to college, one of the things that would push me out of bed before I went to sleep was knowing that I had to get down on my knees and pray. I was talking to God all day—"Please just get my father through the day," and everything would be fine.

The experience of all African-Americans has been a biblical one. My dad said that our river Jordan was the Mississippi River, and when you look at the miracles, at all of the things that we as a people have been through in America, you can't help but see how real God is.

Attitude is All

A minister I knew had a saying I will always remember. He said that storms are always there, and there are three positions in life—you're either going into a storm, you're in a storm, or you're just coming out of one. But for me, the glass is always half full. I believe the sun is shining all the time. I believe everything in life has its place. Hard times will pass through. I always know that the sun is shining somewhere, and if I just hang in there another 12 hours, I'll see the sun again.

Sylvia's stepping stones to happiness...

Having harmonious relationships is one of the most vital principles to learn. When we meditate, we soften the rough edges of our personality.

CHAPTER 9

Technique—Resurrection Breath and Meadow-Woods-Mountain-Waterfall

For Santita, the image of the shining sun is powerful, returning time after time without fail, bringing spirit and renewing light. Next, I will show you a meditation technique which also uses images from nature.

The Meadow-Mountain-Waterfall technique is soothing; it calms our minds, and relaxes our bodies. This technique helps us address negative emotions like fear, and helps us find comfort. This is also a good time to introduce the cleansing breath, a premeditative step that signals your mind that it is time to step away from the surface world, and go inside.

Resurrection Breath

Use this cleansing breath at the start of any meditation. It is a way to symbolically hit a restart button, letting go as you exhale, and symbolically starting anew as you inhale.

Here is how to do the resurrection breath:

1. Facing forward, inhale deeply through the nostrils

2. Turn the head to the left and exhale forcibly through the open mouth two times

3. Turn the head back to the front and inhale through the nostrils, feeling renewed and in the moment, bringing new focus for your meditation

A variation that is very soothing is to make step three the sipping breath, by pursing your lips as though you're about to drink through a straw. Inhale as long and as slowly as possible, stop before you become uncomfortable, and hold the breath for as long as you can without straining yourself. This is a very cooling breath, and a great way to steady the mind. Either way, the practice begins with the two short audible and deliberate exhalations and ends with the inhalation, or symbolic resurrection.

Meadow-Woods-Mountain-Waterfall

1. Perform the resurrection breath.

2. Sit erect, and again visualize pulling energy from your limbs into your core, drawing the energy to the spine. If you want to perform this technique lying down you can, but be sure to keep the spine straight, the chin slightly lower than the forehead, and your eyes resting towards the bridge of your nose and slightly upward. Stay awake! Let the mind settle and ask yourself, "What am I trying to comfort?"

3. Visualize a meadow. Think of the most beautiful flowers you can imagine or remember—you can smell them in the air, you can feel the air's perfect

temperature, you can hear the birds, and feel the breeze. *This represents a place of natural beginnings, undisturbed by man.* See it and enjoy it in your mind.

4. Move slightly downhill, then down through the woods. The trees are strong and full of life, and they inspire you to be able to face your challenges; to bend but not break in the face of adversity. *This symbolizes the things that will come to the surface in life—the dark things we need to acknowledge, not suppress.*

5. Next, see yourself walk up a mountain. The power of the woods lends you strength, and helps you to rise higher and higher. *Ascending the mountain symbolizes overcoming obstacles and the unconscious mind.*

6. See the beauty of the mountain, and then see a place to rest. It could be a cool cave or a niche— a special light seems to shine down upon it. *The resting place is shrine-like, and represents quiet. The light symbolizes knowledge, awareness, and sanctity.*

7. Observe a waterfall tumbling down. As you approach it, feel the water on your skin washing away all negativity, refreshing and cleansing you. Negativity flows out from your feet, and into the soil. The light detaches you from your physical body as the water washes over and through you, cleansing your mind, body, and spirit.

8. You may visualize rising above the mountain to the highest place imaginable. There you may see the form of your chosen deity, and be at peace.

9. When your mind starts to wander, or when you feel ready, descend the mountain. Return to your physical space, breathing deeply. Bring your awareness back to your body and physical space, but keep the feeling of the meadow, the mountain, and the waterfall with you.

As a Guide to Your Meditation

I find this meditation to be extremely soothing and renewing, but most of all, it reduces fear. When she was young, Santita Jackson feared for her father's safety greatly. A way to conquer this type of fear is by doing an affirmation. One of my favorite teachers, the philosopher and author Wayne Dyer, uses this affirmation which I think is particularly applicable: "My loved ones and I cannot and will not be impacted by the presence of evil anywhere in the world."

Just think about how much fear can be removed if we take this affirmation to heart, every minute of our lives. The stress, the things we don't mean to say, and the negative feelings we attract would all be eliminated. Remember—strive to think positive thoughts.

I know firsthand the power of fear and love, and how the two cannot co-exist. I love the city, but I've known many moments of fear for my children. As parents, we owe it to our children to give them a sense of our love, protection, and our faith that they will be all right. I fought hard to get this optimism back into the light as gangs and crime infiltrated my working class neighborhood. My children helped me get my faith back by challenging me to be the positive person they knew and loved.

As my friend, the young minister Daniel Cooperrider once said in a sermon, "Anxiety adds nothing to the abundance of the day." In the end, what good is worrying? Most of us have heard of the fight or flight response our bodies have when we are faced with a dangerous situation documented by Dr. Herbert Benson. I believe the theory that says that negative and fearful thoughts have a detrimental impact on our bodies.

What is the answer? Settling the mind with meditation, and letting go of worry! With light and love, you can never go wrong. Believe that things happen to you for your *ultimate* good, and believe that this moment is as it should be.

Sylvia's stepping stones to happiness...

---

we are creating tomorrow by what we think, say, and do today—act accordingly!

CHAPTER 10

Ayub Agunbiade

Ayub is an aviation engineer originally from Nigeria, and is a devout Muslim. He finds his joy in ritual, tradition, and culture. This is his story...

I've come to appreciate my religion, but when I was growing up it was hard. My parents, especially my father, always wanted me to do what I did not want to do, or felt I did not have time to do. For example, no matter how late I went to bed the night before, my father would wake me up at five o'clock in the morning to go do prayers at the mosque. This happened every day, and sometimes he would wake me up and just leave, expecting me to follow. A couple of times though, I watched and waited until he left, and then I went back to sleep! One day he forgot something so he came back. He found me sleeping, and whipped me to make me get up. After that, any time my parents got me up, I made sure I went to the mosque.

As I grew up, I came to appreciate the religious discipline that my father had given me. I didn't just continue with Islam because my parents forced me to; I wanted to continue. I was able to study other religions, but I believed in the message brought by the prophet called Mohammed.

A Personal Relationship

Eventually, things that my father taught me started to make sense in my life. I came to see wisdom and good sense in the Koran. I really studied and developed a stronger habit of prayer and observance. I enjoy the discipline of the holy days, of prayer, and of fasting. Traditions that people practiced in the Koran centuries ago are still in existence today. Our ancestors had Ramadan, the 30-day fasting period, and we continue it today. I like that it was there for those before you, and will be there for those who follow. You also see that the prophets, from Abraham to Isaac, Noah, Moses, and Jesus Christ, all had a history of observing their actions, of self-awareness. These factors give me a strong faith, and a connection to our religious celebrations.

Comfort in the Holy Word

When you are a Muslim, you are always encouraged to know how to read some Arabic words and to memorize chapters and the verses in the Koran. This gives me real wisdom that I can use on this earth. It provides me with prayers. There are prayers for when you are depressed, when you are looking for something, when you want to achieve something, or maybe you're traveling and you're just asking for God's protection. For example, I've faced some hard times with others in my job, but when I pray over it, my foe becomes a friend. I think this is because of spiritual reflections that help me to know how to approach a situation. I don't win and they don't lose—we just connect as people.

There was a time when things were very, very disturbing around the airport industry, based on the bad things that had happened; things that people from other countries that are predominately Muslim had done. Some people were very ignorant about the religion itself, and about the political things that were going on between countries, so they acted as if "Muslim" meant "terrorist." Even during this time I was comforted by my prayers, and people were still respectful of my practice. I'd go to the locker room when it was my time for prayers, and people respected this. They also knew that my religion prevented me from eating pork, and they respected that when we shared meals together.

I have found that my spiritual practice attracts friends who are more protective of what I do, as opposed to having negativity or fear. I believe it is because though I may be different from them, my approach to the world reflects the kindness and the real love I've learned from Islam.

I don't regard myself as a full time preacher, but I preach whenever I have the opportunity to talk to people and share. Human beings are the only creation of God's that are able to discern right and wrong, so I always say this—study any religion that makes sense to you, and see what works for you. If they are interested in my faith, I tell them the reasons why I have stuck with Islam—it has worked for me, and makes me a happy man.

I am in love with every church
And mosque
And temple
And any kind of shrine

Because I know it is there
That people say the different names
Of the one God.

—Hafiz (13th century poet)

CHAPTER 11

Technique—Contemplation and "Mouna" (Silence)

My teacher and guru is fond of saying, "God is good, and out of goodness only goodness can come." He adds that God, by whatever name we use, is not angry or jealous, but loving and kind. It is the laws of man that can be the source of pain and misunderstanding. When a religious tradition speaks to your heart, it is a powerful thing. Ayub finds comfort in connection to rituals, and has made following the spiritual practices of Islam a priority in his life. Having practiced his spiritual ritual since he was a boy makes it easy for Ayub to go into a state of meditative prayer. He gets out his prayer rug, closes his eyes, bows down, and is transformed. We may need a little more help crossing from the outer world to our inner realm. This contemplation technique, along with "Mouna," which means silent meditation, can be used to help connect us to ancient rituals of the past.

The Contemplation Technique—Basic Variation

This simple process can almost make meditation as easy as 1, 2, 3! To do the basic version, sit still at attention without tension. Shrug your shoulders a couple of times, and set your intention to go inward and upward. Do your resurrection breath, and begin.

1. Count to five, narrowly focusing on each number. Do this several times rather quickly, without letting other thoughts interfere. 1, 2, 3, 4, 5.

2. When you've accomplished this, repeat it, but go a little more slowly, adding more space between the numbers. 1... 2... 3... 4... 5.

3. Find a pace that allows you to repeat these steps 5-7 times with your awareness limited to the numbers. Whatever was on your mind should be replaced by total relaxation, and your focus should be on simple recitation. If you get distracted, start again at one. You will find first a method of concentration, and then second a method of contemplation, and finally a method of meditation, wherein your mind is focused on one point at a time.

4. Take a deep breath, hold as long as comfortable, and let it out as slowly as possible. Observe how you feel.

The Contemplation Technique—Advanced Variation

You may increase the effectiveness of this mind-settling meditation by incorporating your breath. Long-time meditators might actually find this method to be easier than the first, if breath control is a regular part of their practice.

1. Don't do anything with your breath other than observe it. Mentally count *one* as you breathe one full breath. Inhale *one*, exhale *one*. Inhale *two*, exhale *two*, and so on.

2. Follow your natural breathing pattern. Don't force the breath in or out.

3. If your mind wanders, gently and without judgment start again.

4. If you take a long time to get to five, that's okay! If you can reach and sustain the count to five, you can increase to a higher number, like eight or ten. Repeat 5-7 times.

With both versions of the technique, the goal is to settle your mind; to find a peaceful, harmonious, and pleasant space where your body is simply breathing. You will find that there will become longer and longer pauses between the inhalation and exhalation. Now you're on the road to true bliss.

"Mouna" Silence

There are times when I look back and realize that what I said at a meeting, to my kids, to a friend, or to a stranger was out of line, rude, or ignorant. I know there are times when I can approach the world from my highest self, but there are other times when just plain insensitivity gets the best of me. It happens to all of us, but the good thing is that we can reflect on what happened (Tarka) and forgive ourselves; we can learn and move on. When I see a pattern of being a bit of a motor mouth, I like to try a period of Mouna. I'm a big fan of this technique!

1. Select a time when you will be able to go a half a day, or 24 whole hours, without speaking.

2. It is ideal to be in a setting like a retreat, but I've vacationed with understanding friends who respected my choice to spend one day in silence.

3. You don't pass notes or do sign language. You refrain from talking on the phone, e-mail, and texting.

4. Use the time to be thoughtful—see what comes up from your subconscious, and use your Tarka technique.

5. This is a great time to journal, to draw, to be creative and self-aware.

6. Of course if someone's safety is a factor you must speak, but you'll be surprised at how far a smile and a nod can get you!

7. You might still take meals with others and be present, or you might try adding solitude to your practice instead.

8. If you can't manage a full day remember that you can be silent at least a few minutes every day during meditation.

Reminders for Mouna

- Silence helps us see what our real issues are.
- Silence exposes the fact that much of what we say is in defense.
- The more insecure we are, the more we chatter.
- Not talking can make others uncomfortable, so it is important to be kind—share what we are doing or find a time when we will not inconvenience others.
- Remain silent, but if you absolutely must come into contact with others, adapt and adjust—people come first.

As a Guide to Your Meditation

It should be possible, and in fact it is desirable, to integrate a meditation practice into your daily routine without making a big show of effort, or upsetting the household applecart. There is no need to make a big announcement: "I AM ABOUT TO MEDITATE! GIVE ME PRAISE AND ATTENTION!" There is no need to get flighty. Meditation should help us in our everyday world. Martina, a fellow meditation teacher, remarked upon how much her life improved with meditation, and how she was better able to handle her duties as a wife, mother, and human being. As my teacher says, we should "keep one foot on earth as we seek the heavens." He also advises that when you are done meditating, you should do something nice like wash the dishes or run an errand. The benefits of your practice will show in how you live your life, and the people around you will benefit.

Meditation should be a joy, not a job or a hurdle to overcome. If you only meditate five minutes a day, that's fine. If you have 30 seconds of bliss, it is worth hours of rest.

Sylvia's stepping stones to happiness...

Happy people see some connection between themselves and the divine, between their individual lives and the universe.

CHAPTER 12

Mary Whitney

Mary finds joy in her work as an astrologer, her marriage, and her practice of Kriya yoga. This is her story...

I was brought up Roman Catholic, which was extremely helpful to me growing up. My nature is devotional, and Catholicism makes that very easy. We spent many hours in school studying religion, and in the fourth grade my teacher let us actually act out the gospel. She was a very old nun, but quite liberated for the time, seeing as she allowed the girls in the class to play Jesus. One of the highlights in my life at that point was that I got to play Jesus walking on water.

My life was not easy, and I found solace in the church and the lives of the saints. Catholicism taught me a sense of unselfishness, and the importance of service. I was the second oldest child-the first daughter, and there was strife and alcohol abuse in my family. There was mental stress and some physical violence as well. I was always trying to figure out why we were so dysfunctional.

To me, it seemed that the highest calling for a Catholic was to serve, and I felt called upon to serve my family. When I was 13 the church began telling us that everything they had taught us from first to eighth grade was symbolism, like Santa Claus. I started to have doubts, and stopped going to church on my own. I had lost my faith. I was not happy, because it had been easier to have a belief system and feel devotional. The years between me losing the Catholic faith and meeting my husband were very bleak for me. I did not feel that there was anything greater for me to aspire to.

When my husband Gary introduced me as a young adult to the philosophy of yoga; each one of us creating our life rather than adhering to an organized religion, it felt so easy yet so profound. I sat in his backyard one summer day, and it seemed like the world opened up to me finally. I learned about Karma, and it helped me to understand my family. Yoga gave me answers. Now there is no question that meditation is the absolute foremost blessing in my life. It is the thing that has helped me more than anything else. Going inside myself and finding balance brings me happiness.

Astrology and Yoga

Astrology fits right in with my practice of yoga. Astrology is an ancient science and art. Your astrological chart is your "map," allowing you to foresee situations that are going to be challenging for your mind. The more you learn about it, the more it can help you in your day-to-day life. This is easy to see, because it is linked to the moon. The moon changes position every two and a half days. There is a new moon, a full moon, and so forth. Through the moon, you can see rough spots coming, and try ahead of time to balance them out. If you know it, you can change it. Every single day I know where the moon is, and I know what it's doing in my chart. Many people have asked me to pick their wedding date, or decide when they should start a business. That's called electional astrology. Ancient people have always done this, and now, in the modern world, we're going back to it.

A Joyful Life

When I was growing up, I was extremely serious. I had a serious upbringing, and I had a lot of responsibilities. I did not allow myself to think about being happy. I found meditation and Hatha Yoga before astrology, and they're all happily mixed together now, giving me a map for my life and techniques to control my mind. I can say that life is absolutely fabulous, every single moment! I love it. I'm just ecstatic about living, and this confidence in life and balance has come from astrology, Kriya yoga, and meditation. They make me happy every day.

The Sun never said to the Moon 'you owe me.'
Look what happens with a love like that,
It lights up the whole sky!

—Hafiz (13th century poet)

CHAPTER 13

Technique—
New Moon Journal and Fasting

Awareness of the movement of the planets and astrology are central to Mary Whitney's spiritual life. You may not know how the planets are aligned on any given day as Mary does, but it is relatively easy to incorporate the lunar cycle into your life. Contemplating the big, beautiful, ever-present moon reminds us that we are part of the miracle of life beyond our cares and woes. Many standard calendars still show the cycles of the moon, even if most people don't notice them, or know what they are for.

The phases of the moon are counted in quarters. The new moon is the first, and is around two weeks after the full moon. It is when what we see of the moon from the earth is the first sliver. Here is a process for you to try during that time.

New Moon Meditation Journal

This period is a wonderful time for new beginnings, or to be extra reflective. The sages say to be very mindful of the choices we make and the actions we take when the moon is new, because what happens on the new moon is repeated when the moon is full, or that what is begun on the new moon comes to fruition when it is full. You can see if this is true for yourself with a new moon journal.

Here is how to keep a New Moon Meditation Journal:

1. The day before the calendar says a new moon is coming, do a bit of Tarka or reflection, and write down your thoughts about your day.
2. Continue this practice for the two weeks or so between the new and full moon.
3. Be honest with yourself as you capture your mood and the major events of the day, as well as the feeling of your meditation. Gauge what I call your "feeling state"—were you quickly calmed and your mind easily focused? Or were you more distracted on a given day, needing more time to reach a place of contentment? If possible, write in your journal after your meditation, when your mind is clear. But if you can't, just capture the key points anytime during this day.

Test the theory of the new moon/full moon connection. Did the new moon find you mellow, with things going your way? If so, was this pleasant state of affairs repeated on the full moon? Or were you crabby and plagued by little pieces of misfortune at the new moon, and again at the full moon?

Most people have heard of the so-called "full moon effect," when the world seems a little crazier, and weird stuff tends to happen. However, few of us understand how actions at the new moon might play a part in these outcomes. The new moon is a time to set our intentions for the next few weeks. The lesson here is to only do that which is good for you, so that there will be a better chance for you to be happier and more content.

A moon meditation journal is a wonderful stepping stone on the path to enlightenment. If you start the journal with the new moon, and then read it on the full moon, you can learn a lot about what is going on in your subconscious. This is not only a wonderful tool for self-awareness and all the benefits it brings, but you can also see for yourself if the new moon/full moon connection is true!

New Moon Food Fasting

A friend and fellow meditation teacher, Zsolt, swears by fasting as a way to stay healthy. He thinks that when he fasts, the energy normally spent digesting food is instead dedicated to boosting his immune system. At least once a week he eats a breakfast of fruit, and then takes only liquids the rest of the day. If you'd like to try fasting, you can start by just giving up a meal, or by fasting one day a week. I fast by taking in only liquids from the night before the new moon, until sundown or six o'clock in the evening— whichever comes first—the next day.

There are numerous books you can read about fasting, and before you try it you should consult with a healthcare professional. However, I do have a few tips to share, as it relates to your meditation practice:

- Fasting helps us understand the concept called *Neti Neti Neti*—"I am not this body, I am not this mind, I am not this thought," because it reminds us that though our body feels hunger, we are more than that.

- Fasting not only helps us realize that most of us can get by with eating less, it also takes us to the threshold of the inner and outer worlds, and helps us to see what is truly real, and really important by helping us get past thoughts of our immediate physical desire.

- Whether fasting or not, the sages say we should eat like a prince in the morning and a pauper at night. In other words, eat our larger meals in the daytime. This will give you more energy when you are active and need it, and time to digest your food before you go to sleep, to make sure that your body has time to rest and renew.

- When you feel a hunger pang while fasting, use it as a cue to be grateful of your awareness of *this* moment, and your effort to connect to something greater than yourself.

As a Guide to Your Meditation

I believe that the moon is an ever present reminder of the vastness, wonder, and beauty of this Universe in which we are all connected. Using the reliable new moon as a time for special reflection, affirmation, and even forgiveness, is a great "celestial appointment" to make and keep with yourself. It is setting an intention to be conscious of your connection to all of Life. In a world where we are all connected in some way to television, mobile phones, iPods, and other *external* stimuli, I find it to be humanizing and uplifting to connect to the moon, which is a powerful force of nature, but also a reminder of our *internal* spiritual landscape.

Sylvia's stepping stones to happiness...

---

*Wake up! It is never too late to wake up, ana-
lyze who we are, and what our real work is. It
is never too late to be what we are meant to be,
and after that, it is never too late to dream a
new dream and do it all over again!*

CHAPTER 14

Sharon Carlson

Sharon Carlson is a professional actor, singer, educator, writer and practicing Catholic. She finds her joy in music, both during worship and in her life's calling. Sharon also gains inspiration from affirmations and setting intentions. This is her story...

My parents had six children, and we six were raised Catholic, in spite of some opposition from my father's side of the family. My parents married after only dating two weeks, and their families were less than happy with their choice of mates. They were married for over 50 years when they passed, so it seemed to work. My husband is a non-Catholic, or, as he calls it, he's "a fallen-away Presbyterian." He is, however, a very kind, spiritual man, and feels no need for an organized religion. While dating he was impressed by my strong Catholic faith. We'd start our weekly date right after I went to Saturday Confession. He always expressed admiration for the "peaceful look of forgiveness" on my face as I exited the confessional. He said that I glowed with a peaceful expression. He was right. I sincerely believe in the Sacrament of Confession and its forgiveness.

We were married in the Catholic Church, however, outside the communion rail. During our Pre-Cana studies with the priest before we married, my husband confessed that he appreciated the faith, but he couldn't accept it as his own. He especially found the part about the Holy Ghost hard to believe. Father smiled and gently retorted, "Me too."

My faith has been a strong influence in my life, and my husband and I raised our children Roman Catholic. After our last child graduated from college I relaxed my own strict adherence to Sunday Mass attendance. I felt that since I didn't have to get the kids to church anymore, I could spend some Sunday mornings in communion with God while peacefully walking along the lakeshore with my husband.

Practicing Gratitude

I have an affirmation that I say every morning religiously: "I am alive, alert, energized, and something wonderful is going to happen today. "I say that before I even know if I *can* get out of bed. And what is lovely is that something wonderful *does* happen every day. Now, it's not always an earth-shattering thing, but something exciting and reaffirming, like learning a new word, or receiving a phone call from a dear friend, learning a new recipe, or meeting a new person. Whatever comes, this affirmation gives me the focus to accept what happens in the day. It gives me the optimism to begin the day.

Unfolding Inner Beauty

I had rheumatic fever when I was 6, and was bed-ridden for a year. I was not allowed to exercise, so I consoled myself with food. One lovely day my parents surprised me and bought a piano. That was the gift that awakened something incredible inside of me. Music freed me in many ways. I loved to sing and play the piano and would do so for hours... and... I looked good sitting in front of the piano! I was the pianist at school events all through elementary and high school. I still had esteem problems. Brad, an elementary school "friend," helped to keep that problem fresh. He played and sang to me the "She's Too Fat For Me" Polka at school parties.

When I met my husband, he also had esteem problems. We were in our late teen years. He was the kid with the glasses and the briefcase that was only five feet tall as a high school freshman, and then experienced an awkward 10-inch growth spurt. I was the chubby girl that didn't fit in with the "in" girls. On our first date, Richard and I talked until five in the morning. It was amazing how we just fit together. To this day, even when we argue (we're both very passionate souls), we're always best friends.

Unfolding Hidden Talent

We married after college and moved on with dreams of a house in the suburbs, three children, a dog, and a station wagon. I achieved them by thirty, now what? I taught 6th grade but my music was missing. I loved to sing, but a professor in college had told me that my voice was not lovely enough for a career in music, so I stopped singing. But I felt that I had a singer inside that needed to "come out."

I loved to sing and play piano and wanted to pursue a career in music, but I knew I was a "big girl," not fit for the stage. I was affected by all the male put-downs while growing up. Then I met a woman who freed me. A new voice teacher encouraged me to pursue a career as an opera satirist. She said, "What do you mean you're big? Have you ever seen the Broadway and opera stars that are big girls?" She opened my eyes. My voice teacher opened the door and pushed the singer in me out. My husband had always encouraged me, so now with their urging and support I was unstoppable.

I wrote a one-woman show in six months: "Sharon Carlson in Concert" and brought in a huge audience! I wrote and performed stand-up comedy in Las Vegas, but realized that I wasn't a tough, Vegas broad. I used my experience as an elementary teacher and wrote a motivational program entitled, "I'm a Recovering Burned-Out Teacher" and went on tour.

Richard balanced his job with watching the kids, and I started a whole new career as an educational lecturer. My lectures started and ending with songs…and I got my audience singing. Incredible! I did that for many, many years. I also started a singing telegram company called "Gram-Crackers."

By chance I was "discovered" singing in a gay club. Two writers asked, "Would you mind if we wrote a show for you?" It had happened! I had so much support, and I finally had the confidence to move on! I thank God for it every day. I have performed on stage in musical comedy and theater for 30 years. I'm so grateful. Before I perform, I always pray and thank my parents for their gifts. I don't pray for stardom… I only ask God to help me remember the words!

Words to Live By

Once I found my passion— communication through singing— I couldn't stop. Now, even now, at my "certain age," I find new adventures every day. When a new challenge comes along, I don't say no, I say let me think about it, I'll try it. When you take a risk, you always open the door for something new, even if you don't always succeed.

I say follow your dreams and keep your heart open. When I grew up, the priest turned his back on the entire congregation during the Mass, and it was difficult to entirely relate at all to what was going on. Now it is better. We relate to each other in my favorite Vatican II adaptation through the "Kiss of Peace," wherein the congregants shake each other's hands, and idealistically share the word through the physical contact. I find it a time to see the best of people.

In worship I want to be fancy, but that doesn't mean in my clothes—it means in my attitude. I am happy to sing in church because Sister Mary Catherine told me years ago, "You sing once, and if it's in church, you pray twice." So I always feel when I sing in church, I'm reaching God, and the people. I think when we're in church, any church, there is good energy going up to God to thank him for where we are now.

Sylvia's stepping stones to happiness...

See yourself as connected to everyone, because while it can be tough to relate to others, it is through them that we learn and grow.

CHAPTER 15

Technique—Practicing Gratitude and the OM Mantra

Practicing Gratitude

Sharon starts her day with good thoughts and a positive attitude. One technique you can use to do this is to spend a week being conscious of all that you are grateful for.

1. Notice the thought that comes to mind when you ask yourself what you have to be grateful for.
2. Write this thought down on a piece of paper and save it somewhere.
3. Do this for a week and then look at what you have written.
4. Make a list of all that you were grateful for and come back to it when you need inspiration and joy.

Another technique is called **Okagesamade**(O-ka-geh- sa-ma-deh.) This is a Japanese technique of deliberate and specific gratitude towards the people who help make your world possible.

Gratitude towards:

1. Your parents
2. The people who built the house you live in
3. Those who created the streets you walk on
4. The farmers who grow the food you eat
5. The people who make the clothes you wear
6. Continue this thinking with genuine feeling, filling in what matters to you until you have 9 or so points of appreciation

The technique can be broad or specific, but the bottom line is, "I can be happy because of you!"

Okagesamade is a reminder of our interdependency, as well as another way to send joy to the world—and I believe that the joy you send to the world comes back to you 100-fold!

Mantra

Sharon Carlson feels the joy of worship when she is singing, and many faith practices from ancient times began with sound. Sound is a primary mechanism of creation. Mantra is sacred energy-based sounds used to quiet the mind so that the true inner voice can be heard. On a practical level, Mantra helps to quiet the body in the same way as observing the breath does. If you can join me in believing that what we think can impact what we do, then you can see the benefit of wrapping the mind around a concept or positive thought form, and saying it over and over again.

As a Guide to Your Meditation

OM is the great mantra and the universal sound. The ancient Hindu text, the Upanishads, have this to say about OM: "Whatsoever has existed, whatsoever exists, whatsoever shall exist hereafter is OM. And whatsoever transcends past, present and future, that is also OM."

OM is well known enough to be a cliché—when one says, "I practice meditation," the reaction is often a smile and the sound "Ommmm." From sitcoms to cartoons, it is a concept that resonates in popular culture, and that's okay!

OM is pronounced like "Home" without the "H" which the Upanishads describe as "AUM."

OM Mantra with Exhalation Breath

1. Sitting upright, inhale with a sense of taking the breath down to the base of the spine.
2. OM can be thought of as comprised of three letters, A-U-M, forming three phases or syllables. Go deep into the sound to hear it physically and mentally. Then sense a fourth level, a Self, indivisible and beyond the words.
3. Open the lips and make the OM sound while exhaling slowly. Try to make a continuous sound for as long as you can, with the "A" taking up most of the time. When you feel 90% done—before you become uncomfortable—express the "U-M" with the last part of your breath.
4. Inhale with the breath, going down the spine again, and repeat. Empty the mind and let the "feeling state" of the sound envelop you.

6. Combining mantra with a mental intent increases its effect. But again, just the repetition of the sound is effective.

7. On your last breath inhale deeply, hold a few seconds, exhale as slowly as possible.

Mantra Overview

OM is the reflection of all that was, all that is, and all that will ever be in the end. The OM mantra is the ultimate reminder of the "big picture," that we are more than our fears, our concerns, and our aches and pains. This sound is the sound of eternity, and it tells us that we are a perfect part of the Universe.

Sylvia's stepping stones to happiness...

Remember, it is not what happens, but how one reacts to it that impacts one's life.

CHAPTER 16

Derrick Baker

Derrick Baker's daughter Danielle was killed by a drunk driver in an automobile accident one month short of her 22nd birthday. She left behind a two-year-old daughter, Jasmine. Derrick experienced the worst thing that can happen to a parent, but his general faith makes him resilient, optimistic, and leaves room for joy in his world. This is his story...

During my youngest years, I grew up in the Holiness religion, which is a southern religion linked closely to the Baptist beliefs, centered on immersion baptism. Then we were Lutherans; when I was about ten years old my family converted, and of course, I went along with it. You know, at that age, you did what your parents told you to do, but as a child I enjoyed the service at the Holiness church more than I did at the Lutheran church, because the Holiness church was a little more joyous in spirit, and the Lutheran church was a little more conservative.

I can't say I'm as deeply religious as a lot of people are, but I can say that growing up in both churches definitely shaped who I am today. It formed my basic beliefs on how to treat my soul, and it's kept me going. It has given me faith in the fact that everything is going to work out, no matter what it is—belief in a higher power does do that for a person.

I have had to face what no parent ever wants to see happen, yet I do have faith in God. I believe that He does know what is best, and He is not going to give me anything that I can't handle. Even though something may be painful at the time, I believe I can persevere.

I know that I have a responsibility to my grandchild Jasmine, and I have a responsibility to myself. When you lose a loved one, you also have a responsibility to them. They would want you to keep going, and to persevere and pursue whatever goals you had before the tragedy happened.

Advice for Living

To anybody going through a tragic loss, my advice is this— to stay as close to who *you* are as you can. I know that there is something that will never be the same, but I try to be as much of Derrick Baker as possible. I like to think that in my heart I've forgiven this drunk driver. I've continued to uphold my family, and to raise my granddaughter. I believe you never should give up. No matter how bad it is, there is life left within me, and therefore Danielle will live through me. The days we have allotted to us may be a mystery, but we have a choice about how we use the time. I have learned that you are better off being forgiving, loving, and hopeful no matter what, because life will always continue, even when you think you can't go on.

Sylvia's stepping stones to happiness...

Your attitude towards life is not determined by God or Guru but by you.

CHAPTER 17

Technique—The Story of Frederick and the Happiness Memory Bank

Derrick Baker has maintained a positive attitude, even in light of an immense tragedy. There are ways to lift our spirits that are as simple as looking up to the vastness of the sky and feeling our connection to the wonders of the Universe, letting the healing energy of the sun's light gently touch our awareness.

The Story of Frederick

I take great inspiration from a story by children's author Leo Lionni—the story of Frederick, the mouse. During the summer, Frederick sits quietly absorbing the sun and the colors, the sights, sounds, and smells. In the fall, when the other mice are preparing their nests for winter, he still spends his time enjoying the beauty of the days instead of gathering nuts and seeds and hay. A young mouse notices this, and asks his mother why Frederick doesn't work. His mother replies, "Oh, he is working. Wait, you'll see."

Winter comes and the mice are prepared, but as time goes by the days get colder, and the stores of food start to dwindle, as do the spirits of the little mice. Then in the heart of their winter, Frederick goes to work. On cold and gray days he shares stories of blue skies, the reflection of sun on the lake, and the beauty of the fields. His memories are so strong, the other mice can feel the heat of the sun on their faces, and they are warmed. He shares his memories of summer feasts and bountiful food, and the mice forget their hunger, and so they are sustained until spring returns.

I urge you to have a little Frederick within you. Create your own happiness memory bank to see you through the tough times.

As a Guide to Your Meditation

If you observe yourself carefully, you'll notice that there are stages of reaction as you try to meditate:

1. The body is restless, and the mind active.
2. We start to relax the body and mind.
3. We are almost asleep, and very relaxed. Here we must stay awake, but still find that effortless peace.
4. Once we reach a length of time of meditation that we are not yet ready for, we may become physically uncomfortable. Stop before discomfort, and you will want to come back again and again.

A Few Reminders

- It's important to go in to and out of sleep and meditation states slowly, allowing us to have more control of our inner world and our life. It is here that we can let affirmations fill our minds with positive, rather than negative thoughts.

- Have different clothes (loose and comfortable), and a pleasant, peaceful designated space for meditation. Yes gals, lose the bra. Guys—get rid of the tight briefs.

- If a negative thought comes in and is hard to ignore, acknowledge it. Name it (car trouble, kids). After meditation, examine why it came in, and what you can do about it.

CHAPTER 18

Conclusion H.A.P.P.I.N.E.S.S.

What one has done, others can do. Learn from positive examples!

Choose Happiness

Meditation can be your pathway to letting go of stress, and making room inside for more positive thought patterns. It is your route to creating a healthy lifestyle. Whatever your faith practice, whatever your belief, you are connected to the Universe. We are all one. We may take a different path to the top of the mountain, and we may see different sights on our journey, but we are all seeking the same destination: peace, contentment, and a spiritual confidence in our place in the Universe. I'd like to leave you with a few extra tools to build a life of joy and happiness, now using my favorite word, happiness, as a reminder.

H. Home

Create a space of peace and renewal for your meditation practice at home. Whether you have a many-roomed mansion or a simple corner in a cramped apartment, make a space that is soothing and peaceful for you. It could be as elaborate as painting the designated room in your favorite calming colors, or as simple as adding fresh flowers, or the fragrance of your favorite incense. Try to bring in experiences of joy and peace, and the energy will build over time to sustain both you and all who enter your space.

A. Attitude

Attitude is all. You may not be able to control everything that comes into your life, but you do have power to control your attitude towards it. When we are feeling good about ourselves, we overlook slights and inconveniences. When we are in a less positive frame of mind, the smallest thing can set us off. Be the observer, watching your behavior and moods, and use the old trick of saying, "isn't this interesting." This allows you to see without judging; to be aware, but to find detachment and cultivate the ability to keep people, places, and events in perspective. Use breathing and self-awareness to learn to settle down your mind and see situations and circumstances more clearly.

One of my favorite sages of all time has the best advice in this regard. Patanjali, the sage (or sages) who set out the framework for yoga, remains a source of wisdom and joy thousands of years after he left this life. Patanjali said that you only need four keys to open any "lock" in life:

Friendliness towards the happy,
compassion for the unhappy,
delight in the virtuous,
and disregard for the wicked.

How awesome is that?

P. Practice

Meditate, meditate, meditate. Find time for meditation practice every day. Go inside to listen and learn about you, and to let go of attachments and anxieties. Whether it is a regular morning meditation, evening Tarka reflection, or midday renewal, have a moment to breathe, let go, empty the mind, and fill it with love and gratitude. As Mary Whitney, my astrologer friend has told me, "go inside and balance what is unbalanced."

P. Patience

You have a lifetime to reach your goals. By the time your desire manifests, you may find you don't even want the same thing anymore! So focus on cultivating contentment. To quote a Chinese saying, "The Tao does nothing, yet nothing is left undone." A Zen saying also captures the essence of this idea—"Sitting still doing nothing Spring comes." Don't spend time on the future or the past; be ever childlike and absorbed in this moment because the actions you take in this moment, in this eternal now, will determine your future.

I. Intuition

Trust your inner knowing. As you connect with your center and find balance, and as you clear away worldly distractions that generally clutter your mind, you can hear your soul sing. Listen to it to know what to do, and when and how to do it. True inner voice will never incite you to violence, or lead you to harm yourself or another being. When we quiet the mind we are more likely to hear what our subconscious mind has to teach us. We are able to learn about ourselves and learn to be content *now*.

N. Neti Neti Neti

Remember *Neti Neti Neti* is a Hindu concept which means I am not this body, I am not this mind, I am not this thought. It is a vital way to contemplate our world. It allows us to separate from ego and fear. It is a prime tool for detachment. One can still be compassionate, but one need not be in charge of fixing others or the world. We just need to do our best and help people the way *they* want to be helped.

E. Expand

Expand your horizon of awareness. We can easily live our lives every day thinking that we are our work, or that we are limited by our current situation. Have faith that we are all connected in a positive way. Trust in the hidden virtue that we are all part of the family of the living souls. Have faith that with wisdom and time, all things are possible. See beyond your day-to-day duties, your circle of friends, and the life you've created. See your connection to the Universe, and to the god within us all. See that you are able to change your world by changing your attitude. You can change who you think you are and the story you have created, which is your life. Expand your awareness to be more enthusiastic and wiser, to become a blessing, to be a light-bringer in this life.

S. Silence

Know when to be quiet. Use the technique of Mouna to listen to your soul, to reconnect to your center and to find balance. Also, use silence and literal physical stillness to check in with yourself when you have a burning passion to take the lead, or when your ego just wants to be heard. Use silence to keep yourself from giving advice unless you've been asked for it several times, and even then say only what is true or what is truly kind. When you choose to listen silently to your family, to children, and to co-workers more often, everyone benefits.

S. Soften

Soften the blunt edges of your personality. Soften your gaze. If you look in the mirror and see a permanent frown, that is a symbol of taking yourself and your perceived problems just too seriously. Soften your voice. Be the first to say "I'm sorry," and the first to say "I love you." Bend like a strong tree, and don't worry about perceptions of winning or losing. Practice non-violence in your thoughts and deeds, and remain ready to enjoy sexual intimacy whether you have a partner at hand or not! It is the human condition to be a sexual being, and if you're not willing to use it, you lose it!

Reminders

- Meditation needs to be repetitive to be effective.
- My meditation teacher training texts cite the physiological benefits of meditation over time, including a lowering of the blood pressure, and a settling of the breathing pattern which results in relaxation. Psychological changes include a more peaceful, creative, and optimistic outlook.
- On the emotional front, people and events are less disturbing in direct proportion to our ongoing meditation practice, and we are less fearful and less
- As the Upanishads say: "Perform everyday duties with a cheerful heart and unattached mind." I say make every duty (from giving a major speech, to

taking on a new job, to baking bread, or washing dishes) an 'everyday duty,' and you can't go wrong.

Ultimately the goal is to remove all physiological limitations to happiness, and to realize that the world is a wonderful place—not a perfect place— after all it is populated by us humans, but still wonderful. It is a place of learning and shared experiences. If we have discipline, maturity, and commitment to doing what it takes to be happy, we can see the order in the Universe and the purpose of life. When we settle our minds with meditation, we can bring happiness, comfort, and joy into our lives and into the world around us.

CPSIA information can be obtained at www.ICGtesting.com
Printed in the USA
LVOW101711120912

298543LV00009B/13/P

9 781457 512209